Contents

Early life

Renoir is one of the world's best loved painters. This is probably because his paintings are full of joy and the people shown in the paintings always seem to be happy. Renoir liked people, especially women and children, and this shows in his work.

Pierre-Auguste Renoir was born in Limoges in France in 1841. He was the sixth youngest of seven children. His mother was a dressmaker and his father was a tailor. Work was scarce in Limoges so the family moved to Paris when Renoir was three years old.

◀ **Portrait of Mademoiselle Sicot, 1865**
This is one of Renoir's first paintings. It is a portrait of an actress called Mademoiselle (meaning Miss) Sicot, who was well-known in Paris at the time. She is seated formally, with her hands neatly folded, looking out of the picture. We are shown her face at what is called a three-quarter view – half-way between a side and a front view.

■ *Renoir made this portrait as life-like as possible. For example, Mademoiselle Sicot's face is painted in a clear and detailed way. Later in Renoir's life his style of painting changed a great deal. He chose much brighter colours to paint with and his figures became less clear and more blurred.*

Luncheon of the Boating Party, 1881

Renoir asked some of his friends to pose for this painting. They are eating lunch at a restaurant near the river, on the outskirts of Paris. A warm light falls on the food and the figures. They have all finished eating and drinking, and now chat excitedly with one another. This is one of Renoir's favourite subjects – people, usually his own friends, having fun.

Cover: Girl with a cat, 1876

End paper: detail from Le Moulin de la Galette, 1876

Paintings in this book are identified by their title followed by the artist who painted them. If no artist is named the painting is by Pierre-Auguste Renoir.

This book was prepared for Macdonald Young Books Ltd by Tucker Slingsby Creative Services London House 66–68 Upper Richmond Road London SW15 2RP

Project Editor: Jackie Fortey
Picture Researcher: Liz Eddison
Design concept by M&M Design Partnership
Designer: Steve Rowling
Artwork: George Fryer, Bernard Thornton Artists

Subject Adviser
Professor Arthur Hughes
Department of Art, University of Central England, Birmingham

A catalogue record for this book is available from the British Library

ISBN 0 7500 1568 3

First published in Great Britain in 1996 by Macdonald Young Books Ltd 61 Western Road Hove, East Sussex BN3 1JD

© 1996 Macdonald Young Books Ltd

Printed in Portugal by Ediçoes ASA

Acknowledgements
t = top; b = bottom; l = left; r = right
Bridgeman Art Library: Front Cover: National Gallery of Art Washington; Front End Paper: John Hay Whitney Gallery; Title Page: Musée d'Orsay, Paris; Phillips Collection Washington 4, 20; National Gallery of Art Washington 6; Musée d'Orsay, Paris 7t, 7b, 17t, 26, 29t; Museo De Arte, Sao Paulo 8; National Gallery, London 11t, 21b, 25; Private Collection 11b; Christie's, London 12, 24t; Wallraf-Richartz Museum, Cologne 13t; Private Collection 13b; Private Collection 14; Courtauld Institute 15, 19; John Hay Whitney Collection 16; Narodni Gallerie, Prague 17b; Metropolitan Museum of Art, New York 18; Museum of Fine Arts, Boston 21t; National Museum of Wales, Cardiff 22; Philadelphia Museum of Art 24b; Private Collection 27; Giraudon 28; Lauros-Giraudon 29b.

Musée d'Orsay/Reunion des Musées Nationaux 10.

The Museum of Fine Arts Boston/Juliana Cheney Edwards Collection 23.

Statens Konstumeer 9.

Tom Parsons

An introduction to
Pierre-Auguste
Renoir

Portrait of Renoir, Bazille 1867

MACDONALD YOUNG BOOKS

When he was 13 Renoir left school to help earn money for his family. His parents found him a job painting porcelain vases and plates. Renoir was very good at this work. However, by the age of 19, Renoir had decided that he wanted to become an artist. With money that he had saved he paid to study at art school.

▲ Portrait of Monet, 1875 (detail)
When Renoir was a young art student, he met the painter Claude Monet, who was to become a lifelong friend. They were both studying at the studio of a Swiss painter called Charles Gleyre. This is a portrait Renoir painted of Monet some years later.

▶ Portrait of Renoir, Bazille 1867
Another friend Renoir made as an art student was Frédéric Bazille. Bazille painted this portrait when Renoir was 26 years old. The way Renoir is sitting, with his legs drawn up on the chair, and the alert expression in his eyes, tell us something of his nervous, energetic character.

Off to the forest

While Renoir was studying in Paris, he would spend hours looking closely at the work of other artists in museums. At other times he enjoyed going off to paint with his friends in the nearby forest of Fontainebleu. Fontainebleu had been a popular place to visit for some years, especially for city dwellers who wanted to escape to the countryside.

◀ **Le Coeur in Fontainebleu Forest, 1866**
Renoir probably painted this landscape in the forest. His artist friend Jules Le Coeur posed for him.

■ *It is a very thickly painted picture. Renoir used a kind of flat knife, rather than a brush, to apply the paints. As a result the texture as well as the colours of the paint appeal to the eye. This technique is called 'impasto'.*

◀ **The Inn of Mother Anthony, 1866**

The white poodle, Toto, belonged to Renoir's friend Le Coeur. According to Ambroise Vollard, one of Renoir's picture dealers, Toto had a wooden leg! The girl serving food is Mother Anthony's daughter Nana. The man reading a newspaper is Renoir's friend, the painter Alfred Sisley. Some artists who stayed at Mother Anthony's drew cartoons of their friends on the dining room wall. You can see one by Renoir in the top left hand corner of this painting.

■ *Renoir has paid a lot of attention to the hands of his figures. This is because hands can tell us about a person's mood or feelings. The right hand of Sisley (the man with the newspaper) is lively. Monet's hand burrows in a pouch for some tobacco. Nana's hands, gripping the bowls, are red from her work.*

The new railways made the journey to Fontainebleu inexpensive and quick. While he was in Fontainebleu, Renoir would stay at the house of a friend of his called Jules Le Coeur, or he would hire a room at an inn. Many artists stayed at an inn run by a woman they called Mother Anthony.

In the forest Renoir spent his time painting landscapes, something he could not do in his studio in Paris.

Friends

Renoir came from a poor family who could not afford to support him and at first he found it difficult to sell his paintings. Friends would lend him money or give him paints and canvas. Jules le Coeur was particularly generous. Even so, Renoir had to go without food sometimes.

Along with his friend Claude Monet, Renoir began to experiment with painting in a new style. These paintings were even less likely to sell, but Renoir and Monet bravely carried on with their experiments. They were looking for new ways of using colour. Renoir and Monet were also unusual because they liked to paint landscapes in the open air. Most artists at that time sketched outside, but finished their paintings in a studio.

Bazille, who was quite wealthy, remained a good friend to Renoir and Monet. He helped and encouraged them and even shared his studio with them. Sadly he died in 1870 in the war between France and Prussia.

◄ **Studio in the Rue Condamine, Bazille 1869**
In this painting Renoir is seated on the table in the bottom left corner. Monet is smoking, standing behind the painter Edouard Manet, who is looking at a picture on the easel. The other figure in this central group is Frédéric Bazille in whose studio the scene is set. The journalist, Emile Zola, is seen standing on the steps and Edmond Maître, another friend, is playing the piano.

▶ Bathers at La Grenouillère, Monet, 1869
▼ La Grenouillère, 1869

Renoir and Monet liked to paint pictures of everyday subjects, not stories from the bible or mythology, which had been popular with artists in the past. They painted scenes in the country and in the city. La Grenouillère (meaning the 'Frog Pool') was a popular bathing place on the River Seine near Paris. They also used much brighter, stronger colours than artists had used before.

■ Renoir and Monet did not mix their colours together before painting them onto the canvas. They put them down pure and unmixed, in order to make the colours as bright as possible. This was because they wanted to be able to paint all the different effects light can give. Light is often very bright and it moves or flickers quickly.

Impressionism

Renoir and a number of his painter friends used to meet in a café in the north of Paris. They would go in the evening and talk about their work. Their discussions were often very lively. Soon they were joined by others including writers and journalists.

Renoir, and some of his fellow painters who had begun to experiment with brighter colours, had trouble selling paintings. So they decided to hold their own exhibition in the centre of Paris. It took place in 1874. They kept the exhibition open late into the evening to encourage people leaving work to look in on their way home.

One journalist described the paintings as 'impressions'. He meant the paintings were not detailed copies of a view or person. Instead the artists tried to recreate the impression or effect a place or person had on them. In time Renoir and his friends became known as the Impressionists.

◀ The Seine at Chatou near Argenteuil, Monet, 1873

▶ The Seine at Argenteuil, 1873

In 1873 Renoir went to stay with Monet in a house he had rented in the small town of Argenteuil, near Paris. The two painters often worked side by side. Years later Renoir and Monet sometimes couldn't remember who had painted which picture! At this point their paintings did look very similar.

▶ The Sisley Couple, 1868

Renoir met the painter Alfred Sisley while they were both students. Sisley helped Renoir as a young artist when his savings had run out. Renoir shared Sisley's house until Sisley got married. It was on this occasion that Renoir painted this affectionate double portrait of Sisley and his wife. Sisley was another of the Impressionist painters.

■ *There is something very warm in the way that the couple lean towards each other. Renoir has placed their entwined arms just above the centre of his picture. It was unusual at that time to paint portraits out of doors. But because Renoir and the other Impressionist painters were interested in the effects of natural sunlight, they almost always chose to paint their subjects outside.*

■ *The Impressionist painters had equipment which had not been available to artists before and this made a difference to the way they worked. New types of brushes made it easier to dab the paint on to the canvas. Paint was available in brighter colours and could be bought in easy-to-carry metal tubes. Lightweight, portable easels also made it far easier to paint outside as artists could now carry their tools with them.*

13

A changing city

By the 1870s, Paris looked very different to how it had in the 1840s, when Renoir was a child. He and the other Impressionist painters recorded the changes in the city.

At the end of the 1840s large parts of the old medieval city were pulled down. Splendid new buildings began to be put up in their place. The city was then drawn together with a grand system of wide streets and avenues.

▲ **Gare du Nord**
The Gare du Nord was one of the main railway stations built in Paris in the 19th century.

◀ **Les Grands Boulevards, 1875**
The title of this painting means 'the wide streets'. These busy, large streets had recently been built in Paris. To the left a seated man reads a newspaper. Two others have stopped to chat, while a woman and three children cross the crowded street. Nothing is quite in focus. The paint has been very lightly flicked or dabbed on to the canvas to create a feeling of bustling movement.

14

▶ La Loge, 1874

The title of this painting means 'the box' which is where some people sit at the theatre or opera. Renoir's brother Edmond posed as the man in this painting. A model whose nickname was 'fishface' posed for the woman.

■ *This painting is set inside, which is unusual for Renoir. Even so, he has taken a lot of trouble to show the light. He has mixed blue into the blacks and whites of the woman's dress. This gives a sense of the brightness of the lights reflecting off the fabric. There is blue too in the shadow on the white shirt of the man behind her.*

Massive train stations were built on the edges of the city and railway lines were constructed to run from Paris to all over France. Street lights, drains and sewers were installed making the city safer and cleaner. New theatres were built and more people could afford to go to them. The number of people living in Paris grew and many people had more money to spend enjoying themselves. The changes in Paris during the 19th and early 20th centuries can be seen in the scenes the Impressionists chose to paint.

Montmartre

At the beginning of the 19th century Montmartre was a village perched on a hill to the north of Paris. In 1830 it had a population of just 6,000. But by the mid 1880s the population had grown to over 200,000 and it had become part of the city.

Montmartre had many cafés and night-clubs, though it remained a poor area. Renoir moved to Montmartre in the 1870s.

▼ **Ball at the Moulin de la Galette, 1876**
The Moulin de la Galette was a popular dance hall in Montmartre. This is a large painting. Again, Renoir's friends posed for it. They even carried the canvas and easel.

■ *Renoir was beginning to paint his shadows with colour. As he explained himself, 'Shadows are not black; no shadow is black. It always has a colour. Nature knows only colours ... White and black are not colours.' Renoir decided to try to paint without black or white paint.*

◄ **The Swing, 1876**

The Swing, like *Ball at the Moulin de la Galette*, shows that Renoir was very interested in the way shadows look and wanted to show this in his paintings. Here, he was painting the shadows made when sunlight filters through leaves. Spots of yellow light seem to dance on the shady ground. Some of Renoir's friends posed for this painting at the bottom of his garden in Montmartre.

■ *Renoir knew that certain colours only look their best when seen next to certain other colours. Green, for example, looks brightest when placed next to red. For this reason, red and green are known as complementary colours. The same applies to yellow and violet, and blue and orange. Here, Renoir has put in little dabs of orange in the areas of sunlight to make the blues of the shadows more lively.*

For many years Renoir and his family were poor. Then, in the 1890s, he began to earn a reasonable amount of money. However, he and his family continued to live simply. Renoir, for example, wears the same double-breasted tweed coat in many of the photographs taken of him over the years.

▶ **At the Moulin Rouge, Henri de Toulouse-Lautrec, 1892-95**

The Moulin Rouge was Montmartre's most famous night-club. Henri de Toulouse-Lautrec was an artist, younger than Renoir, who also lived in the area. His favourite subjects for painting were scenes of people dancing or sitting in bars and night-clubs there. But where Renoir's people seem happy, those in Toulouse-Lautrec's pictures are rather ugly and strange.

17

The Charpentier family

Paul Charpentier was a wealthy publisher with many rich friends in the most fashionable and elegant circles of Parisian society.

He had bought a picture by Renoir at an auction and decided that he wanted to meet the artist who had painted it. He then paid or 'commissioned' Renoir to paint a portrait of his wife and their two children. This commission came at a good moment. Renoir was still short of money, but he was well paid for this portrait. He received 1,000 francs for it. In Renoir's time, top artists charged up to 100,000 francs for a portrait. However, Renoir was pleased with the amount he received.

Renoir was also able to show the painting at the Salon, the most important exhibition in Paris. Up till then, Renoir and his friends had not been chosen to show their work at the Salon because their paintings were new and different. So this was an important breakthrough for Renoir and the Impressionists.

▼ The Salon

This enormous exhibition was held once a year and visited by thousands of people. The paintings to be shown were chosen by a team of experts, known as the jury. For years the jury did not chose any paintings by Renoir or the other Impressionists. Being chosen by the jury was a great help to artists as they could sell their work at the Salon and try to get new commissions.

▲ Portrait of Ambroise Vollard, 1908

After his success with the Charpentiers, Renoir became well-known as a portrait painter. Many people wanted to sit for him. This portrait is of the art dealer Ambroise Vollard who sold Renoir's works from his small gallery in the centre of Paris. He is shown holding a small statue.

◄ Madame Charpentier and her children, 1876

This portrait earned Renoir some much needed success. Not only was he well paid for it, but it was also well displayed at the Salon. Lots of people would have seen it. Madame Charpentier is wearing a long black dress, and is seated with her two children. The furniture looks slightly Japanese in style – this was very fashionable at the time.

Le weekend

In France, as in most of Western Europe towards the end of the 19th century, working people had more leisure time than ever before.

Boating and swimming were both very popular pastimes at the weekend. The new railways around Paris meant that city dwellers could easily travel to little resorts on the river. Places such as La Grenouillère, Bougival and Le Chatou became just as popular with the Impressionist artists as with holiday makers. Renoir and his fellow artists wanted to paint the lively, everyday scenes of people relaxing.

The busy waterside cafés were excellent subjects for Renoir and the other Impressionists. As well as painting colourful scenes of people enjoying themselves, the Impressionists were very interested in how to show the reflections of light on water. They experimented with new ways to do this.

▶ Dance at Bougival, 1882-83

Bougival was a popular resort for the Parisian public. Renoir's brother posed for this painting along with a model called Suzanne Valadon. Suzanne was also a painter in her own right and later had a child who grew up to be another famous artist, Maurice Utrillo.

◀ Luncheon of the Boating Party, 1881

The Restaurant Fournaise was an open air restaurant on the island of Le Chatou, which lies on the River Seine not far from Paris. Renoir used the restaurant as the setting for this painting. His friends posed for him. In the left corner, Renoir's girlfriend Aline Charigot can be seen holding the dog. Everyone has enjoyed the food and drink, and each other's company.

◀ Bathers at Asnières, Seurat, 1883-4

Seurat was a much younger artist than Renoir. In the 1880s he painted similar scenes to those Renoir had painted before him. But where Renoir enjoyed painting movement and lively exchanges of chatter Seurat's painting seems still and silent.

Travel abroad

When Renoir was in his early 40s he was able to afford to travel. After many years of poverty he had finally begun to sell his paintings.

He made journeys to Italy and Algeria. In Italy he saw the paintings of famous artists from the past. He was very impressed by the work of a painter called Raphael who had worked in Rome in the early 1500s. On his return he went to visit another Impressionist painter and friend, Paul Cézanne, who lived in the south of France. Renoir fell ill and was nursed back to health by Cézanne's mother.

Renoir wrote of her fish stew, 'One should eat this and then die'. In other words it tasted incredibly good!

▲ Mountains at L'Estaque, Cézanne, 1882
◄ Rocky Crags at L'Estaque, 1882

During Renoir's stay with Cézanne at L'Estaque in the south of France the two painters would often walk out into the countryside to paint landscapes. These two pictures were probably made at around the same time. Cézanne later described Renoir's landscapes as 'cottony'. The word sounds a little impolite but Renoir's painting is certainly more loosely and softly brushed than Cézanne's. Where Cézanne's landscape is organised into hard, straight-edged shapes, Renoir's is much more rounded; and where Cézanne's painting seems airless, in Renoir's you can almost feel a warm breeze blowing through the trees and rocks.

In the past, most artists had drawn an outline of their picture on to the canvas and only then put on the paint. For Renoir and the Impressionists, working outside meant that they had to paint quickly before the light changed or it began to rain! They did not draw their figures or landscapes first. They started straight away with the paint.

▶ Renoir and Cézanne
Renoir admired the work of Cézanne and they often painted together. They set up their easels side by side in the open air in the rocky countryside near Cézanne's home.

23

Women

Renoir often chose women as his subjects. He particularly liked painting girls and young mothers. His favourite models were women he knew well. He sometimes used his girlfriends as models, then his wife and later a cousin called Gabrielle who looked after his children.

Sometimes Renoir painted the models nude. This was because he thought that the female body was beautiful. The nude is a subject chosen by many famous artists and Renoir would have seen lots of examples on his visits to the museums in Paris.

▲ Young Girl in a White Hat
This theme turns up again and again in Renoir's work. Renoir enjoyed painting pretty young girls in hats. A straw hat, with a crown of artificial flowers, can still be seen in his old studio.

◄ Bathers, 1883-87
In his earlier Impressionist paintings Renoir had been more interested in light and colour than in line. He had avoided painting contours or outlines around his figures because he wanted to concentrate on the shapes and colours of patches of light and shade falling across the flesh. In later paintings such as *Bathers*, on the other hand, he drew his figures as clearly as possible.

▶ Umbrellas, 1883-84

This work was first shown at the National Gallery in London. A number of British artists wrote to tell Renoir how good they thought it looked among so many other paintings from the past. This was a big compliment.

■ *This painting show both of Renoir's painting styles side by side. The girl on the left is sharply drawn while the mother and her children on the right are much more softly painted. These two women are different in other ways too: one is rich, married and a mother. The other is poor and alone.*

Another favourite theme of Renoir's is hats, framing or half-hiding the face of a girl. The hats give an air of mystery to what might otherwise be a rather ordinary picture. These pretty ladies seem to live in a happy, peaceful world.

Renoir was an artist who liked to show the pleasant, happy sides of life. Some people have criticised him for this and call his work 'escapist', meaning it ignores unpleasant things and escapes into a happy but unreal world.

Family life

▲ Gabrielle and Jean, 1895
Renoir loved painting children, particularly his own. This picture shows Aline's cousin Gabrielle, playing with Jean. Jean was Aline and Renoir's second son. Gabrielle is holding Jean with one hand, while with the other hand she is playing with a toy animal.

R enoir met Aline Charigot in about 1880. She appears in the *Luncheon of the Boating Party* (see page 20) which was painted in 1881. She was the daughter of the shop owner where he normally bought his lunch.

They got married in 1890. They had been living together for five years and had a son, Pierre, born in 1885.

▼ Cagnes
After Renoir became ill, he and his family moved to Cagnes, a pretty village in the south of France. Friends and admirers would travel long distances to watch him paint.

Breakfast at Berneval, 1898

Berneval was the Renoirs' home in Burgundy, in eastern France. It was where Renoir's wife had been brought up as child. They bought the house there in 1898, the same year that this picture was painted. Pierre was 13 and on his school holidays. He is seen in the foreground reading a book. In the background Jean, who later became a famous film maker, talks with Gabrielle.

The Renoirs' second son, Jean, was born in 1894 and their third, Claude, in 1901. In 1898 Renoir suffered his first attack of rheumatism. This is a disease of the bones and it attacked the joints in Renoir's hands. Later, to help his health, Renoir and his family moved to Cagnes in the south of France where the climate is warmer. They bought a farm called 'Les Collettes' and built a house there in an ancient olive grove.

'Les Collettes' became a happy family home. Renoir continued to work, while Aline planted orange trees, grew vegetables and raised chickens.

Illness and old age

In his last years, Renoir's rheumatism made it more and more difficult for him to walk. Eventually he stopped trying to recover the strength in his legs and used a wheelchair or was carried from place to place.

At one point, when he was 56, Renoir broke his right arm in a bicycle accident – so he painted with his left hand until it healed. Despite all this Renoir's later paintings, with their larger-than-life figures, seem full of joy.

▶ **Motherhood, 1916**
Renoir made his first sculptures at the suggestion of the picture dealer Ambroise Vollard. But it was Renoir who decided what he would sculpt. This bronze sculpture is based on a painting Renoir made in 1885.

■ *One way of making or casting a sculpture is to cover a wax model with plaster. When the plaster is hard, the wax is melted and the empty mould filled with hot, liquid bronze. Once the metal has hardened, the mould can be broken open to reveal the sculpture.*

▲ The Great Bathers, 1919

This is one of the very last pictures Renoir painted and one of his best. It was painted just after the end of the World War I. These two enormous women lie happy and relaxed in a warm landscape. Renoir's wife had died a few years before and two of their sons, Pierre and Jean, had been wounded in the fighting, but there is no sense in the painting of Renoir's own personal sorrows. Instead, it seems to breathe out heat, light and a natural kind of joy.

■ *Renoir did not include as much detail in his last paintings as he had done before. The pain and stiffness in his fingers, caused by rheumatism, made it impossible to hold his brush properly. Sometimes he would have the brush strapped to his hand. Renoir changed the colours he used in his later work – he worked with many more reds and fewer greens and blues than in his earlier paintings.*

▼ Photograph of Renoir in his studio, Dornac

This photograph was taken in about 1912, seven years before Renoir's death at the age of 78. Though his hands had become crippled, his eyes still sparkle with vigour.

More information

Glossary

bronze A metal made by combining copper and tin, often used to make sculpture.

canvas Coarse woven cloth used as a surface for painting. First it must be sealed with a coating called a primer and stretched on a frame.

casting A way of making sculpture, by pouring metal (such as bronze), which has been melted down, into a mould and letting it set.

commission This is when a person orders a painting or sculpture from an artist for an agreed fee.

Impressionism A new kind of painting, which began in the 1870s in France. Artists used small dabs of colour to show the effect of sunlight on the appearance of people and objects.

Impressionists Renoir, Monet, Sisley and Bazille were the first Impressionist artists. The group later included Pissaro, Cèzanne, Morisot and Guillaumin, and later Degas and Manet.

medieval Something which dates back to the Middle Ages in history: the time from about AD1000 to 1400.

mythology Collections of stories that have been told and retold, which often try to explain things about the world. Different countries have their own myths.

palette flat board, sometimes kidney-shaped, with a hole for the thumb, used by artists for mixing their colours.

palette knife An artist's tool with a metal blade. Usually used to mix colours on an artist's palette, but is sometimes also used for putting paint on to the canvas.

pigment Paint is made from pigment (colour) and then mixed with either oil or water.

porcelain A kind of fine white china which is often painted in different colours.

Salon Large art exhibition held once a year in Paris.

studio The place where a painter or sculptor works. In Renoir's time, art students would join the studio of a well-known artist to study and learn new skills.

World War I A war lasting from 1914 until 1918, fought mainly in Europe.

People

Frederic Bazille (1841-1870) A popular and talented Impressionist painter, who died in the war between France and Prussia.

Paul Cézanne (1839-1870) French painter, born in the south of France, who became famous for his landscapes, still-lifes and figure paintings.

Claude Monet (1840-1926) One of the leaders of the Impressionists, who painted many landscapes and flower-paintings.

Raphael (1483-1520) A great Italian painter.

Georges Seurat (1859-91) A painter who developed his own style, based on the experiments of Renoir and the Impressionists.

Alfred Sisley (1839-1899) An English Impressionist painter, born in Paris, who painted landscapes.

Henri Toulouse-Lautrec (1864-1901) French painter of life in Paris, best known for his prints and posters.

Emile Zola (1840-1902) French writer and novelist, who was a friend of the Impressionists.